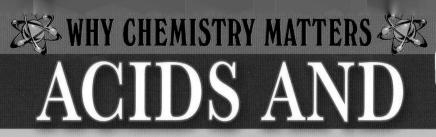

WHY CHEMISTRY MATTERS

ACIDS AND
BASES

LYNNETTE
BRENT

Crabtree Publishing Company

www.crabtreebooks.com

Crabtree Publishing Company

www.crabtreebooks.com

Author: Lynnette Brent
Coordinating editor: Chester Fisher
Series and project editor: Scholastic Ventures
Editor: Adrianna Morganelli
Proofreader: Crystal Sikkens
Project coordinator: Robert Walker
Print and production coordinator: Katherine Berti
Font management: Mike Golka
Prepress technicians:
Margaret Amy Salter, Ken Wright
Project manager: Santosh Vasudevan (Q2AMEDIA)
Art direction: Dibakar Acharjee (Q2AMEDIA)
Cover design: Ranjan Singh (Q2AMEDIA)
Design: Tarang Saggar (Q2AMEDIA)
Photo research: Sakshi Saluja (Q2AMEDIA)

Photographs:
Cover: Science Photo Library/Photolibrary, Christina Richards/Shutterstock (background); Title page: Anyka/Shutterstock; P4: Jmatzick/Shutterstock; P5: Jakub Semeniuk/Istockphoto; P6: BananaStock/Jupiter Images; P7: Greg Pickens/Fotolia; P8: Christina Richards/Shutterstock; P9: Sciencephotos/Alamy (top); P9: Tatyana Nyshko/YinYang/Jovan Nikolic/Istockphoto (bottom); P10: Egidijus Skiparis/Shutterstock; P11: Dragan Trifunovic/Istockphoto; P12: Johanna Goodyear/Shutterstock; P13: Mark Huls/Dreamstime; P14: Laurence Mouton/Jupiter Images; P15: David H. Lewis/Istockphoto; P16: Susan Trigg/Istockphoto; P17: Pamela Moore/Istockphoto; P18: Zergkind/Shutterstock; P19: Tim Mccaig/Istockphoto; P20: Joe Cicak/Istockphoto; P21: Galina Barskaya/Istockphoto; P22: VinceStamey/BigStockPhoto; P23: ooyoo/Istockphoto; P24: Arthur Kwiatkowski/Istockphoto; P25: Icyimage/Shutterstock; P26: Annett Vauteck/Istockphoto; P27: mediablitzimages (UK) Limited/Alamy; P28: Phototake Inc./Alamy; P29: Pavel Drozda/Shutterstock (left); P29: Jim West/Alamy (right)

Library and Archives Canada Cataloguing in Publication

Brent, Lynnette, 1974-
    Acids and bases / Lynnette Brent.

(Why chemistry matters)
Includes index.
ISBN 978-0-7787-4239-5 (bound).--ISBN 978-0-7787-4246-3 (pbk.)

    1. Acids--Juvenile literature. 2. Acids--Basicity--Juvenile literature. 3. Bases (Chemistry)--Juvenile literature. 4. Chemistry--Juvenile literature. I. Title. II. Series.

QD477.B74 2008   j546'.24   C2008-904142-9

Library of Congress Cataloging-in-Publication Data

Brent, Lynnette, 1974-
    Acids and bases / Lynnette Brent.
        p. cm. -- (Why chemistry matters)
    Includes index.
    ISBN-13: 978-0-7787-4246-3 (pbk. : alk. paper)
    ISBN-10: 0-7787-4246-6 (pbk. : alk. paper)
    ISBN-13: 978-0-7787-4239-5 (reinforced library binding : alk. paper)
    ISBN-10: 0-7787-4239-3 (reinforced library binding : alk. paper)
    1. Acids--Juvenile literature. 2. Acids--Basicity--Juvenile literature. 3. Bases (Chemistry)--Juvenile literature. 4. Chemical reactions--Juvenile literature. 5. Chemistry--Juvenile literature. I. Title. II. Series.

QD477.B74 2009
546'.24--dc22
                                    2008028917

Crabtree Publishing Company

www.crabtreebooks.com   1-800-387-7650

Printed in Canada/112014/BF20141015

Published in Canada
Crabtree Publishing
616 Welland Ave.
St. Catharines, ON
L2M 5V6

Published in the United States
Crabtree Publishing
PMB 59051
350 Fifth Avenue, 59th Floor
New York, New York 10118

Published in the United Kingdom
Crabtree Publishing
Maritime House
Basin Road North, Hove
BN41 1WR

Published in Australia
Crabtree Publishing
3 Charles Street
Coburg North
VIC, 3058

Contents

Acid-Base Chemistry   4

What is pH?   6

pH Indicators   8

Properties of Acids   10

Properties of Bases   12

What is a Buffer?   14

Common Acids   16

Acids in Our Bodies   20

Environmental Acids   22

How We Use Bases   24

Chemical Reactions   28

Glossary   30

Index and Web Finder   32

Acid-Base Chemistry

Acids and **bases** are everywhere. If you have a toy that runs on battery power, the batteries have acid in them. When you squeeze a lemon to make lemonade, the juice is an acid. Acids are running through your body, digesting your food, and even building your muscles. What about bases? If you washed your hands today, you probably used soap. Soap is a base.

Acids and bases are just one way to classify **matter**. Matter is anything that has mass, or weight, and that occupies space. Matter comes in three different forms: **solids**, **liquids**, and **gases**. You can only call liquids acids or bases. Almost every liquid that you see has the characteristics of either an acid or a base. A liquid that has more than one substance in it is a **solution**. If you mix baking soda with water, the baking soda dissolves, but the water is changed. The new liquid is a solution. And that solution is basic—has the qualities of a base—instead of acidic, with the qualities of an acid.

An acid is a solution that has many H+ **ions**. *Acid* comes from a word that means "sour." A base has OH- ions. Bases are also sometimes called **alkalis**. In this book, you will read a lot about **aqueous** solutions. An aqueous solution is made mostly of water.

Distilled water has the same amount of positive and negative ions, so water is not an acid or a base. A liquid that is not acidic or basic is **neutral**.

Many acids, like lemon, have a sour taste. Lemon juice is a common acid. Unlike many acids, it is safe to touch.

What is an Ion?

Atoms have three parts: *protons*, *neutrons*, and *electrons*. In most atoms, the number of protons and electrons is the same. If the number is different, the atom becomes an ion. An acid has a hydrogen ion, $H+$. The ion has a positive charge: the ion has more protons than electrons. A base has a hydroxide ion, $OH-$. The ion has more electrons than protons.

What is pH?

The technical definition of **pH** is "potential of hydrogen." An easier way to explain it has to do with the amount of ions in a solution. A compound is a substance made of more than one kind of material. If you place a compound in water and there are a lot of H+ ions, the solution is an acid. Its pH is low. The more H+ ions the solution has, the lower the pH and the more acidic the solution.

If you place a compound in water and end up with a lot of OH- ions, that means that the number of H+ ions is very low. This makes the pH high. The more OH- ions the solution has, the higher the pH and the more basic the solution.

The **pH scale** goes from 0 to 14. The pH of distilled water is seven, right in the middle. Most everyday liquids have a pH close to seven, just a little above or a little below. In a chemistry lab, there are more extremes. A strong acid like battery acid has a pH of less than one. A strong base like drain cleaner has a pH near 14. These chemicals are dangerous to the skin. You need to wear rubber gloves to handle them.

Liquid soap is a base. What do you know about the pH of liquid soap? Remember, the pH of all bases is more than seven.

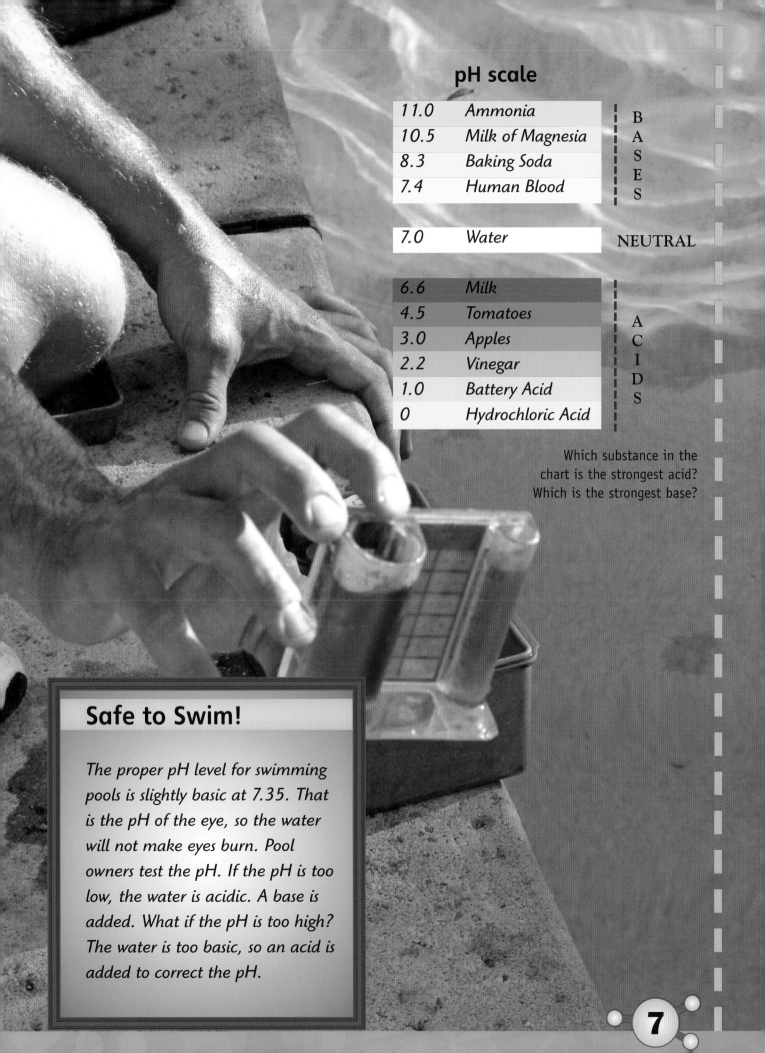

pH scale

11.0	Ammonia	B
10.5	Milk of Magnesia	A
8.3	Baking Soda	S
7.4	Human Blood	E S
7.0	Water	NEUTRAL
6.6	Milk	
4.5	Tomatoes	A
3.0	Apples	C
2.2	Vinegar	I
1.0	Battery Acid	D
0	Hydrochloric Acid	S

Which substance in the chart is the strongest acid? Which is the strongest base?

Safe to Swim!

The proper pH level for swimming pools is slightly basic at 7.35. That is the pH of the eye, so the water will not make eyes burn. Pool owners test the pH. If the pH is too low, the water is acidic. A base is added. What if the pH is too high? The water is too basic, so an acid is added to correct the pH.

pH Indicators

The word *indicate* means "to be a sign of something." An acid-base indicator signals that something is an acid or a base. An acid-base indicator is a weak acid or weak base. An indicator gives a range of pH values. You use it like this:

You have a solution. You add a few drops of thymol blue, an acid-base indicator, to the solution. The thymol blue is an aqueous solution—it is mostly water. If the solution turns red, the solution is an acid. If the solution turns yellow, it is a base. Acid-base indicators do not tell you the exact pH. If you add phenol red to a solution and the solution turns yellow, the solution is an acid. You know that its pH is less than seven. But the indicator doesn't give the exact pH.

Litmus paper is another acid-base indicator. Litmus is made by adding water-**soluble** mixtures of dyes to water and then coating paper with the solutions. These dyes change color in an acid or a base. If red litmus paper changes to blue when dipped into a liquid, the liquid is a base. If blue litmus paper turns red, the solution is an acid. Litmus paper, like acid-base indicators, does not give an exact pH value. To find the exact value, a scientist could use a **pH meter**.

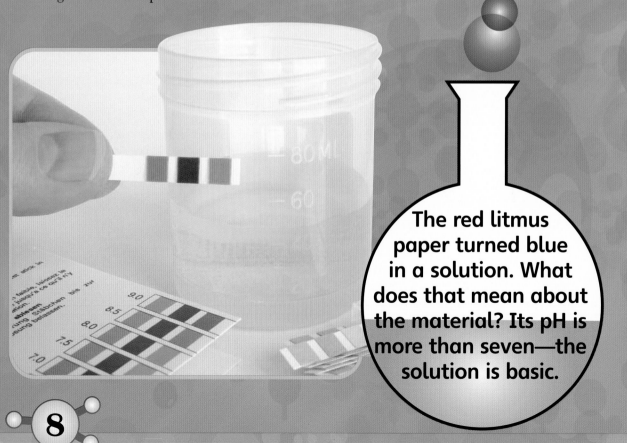

The red litmus paper turned blue in a solution. What does that mean about the material? Its pH is more than seven—the solution is basic.

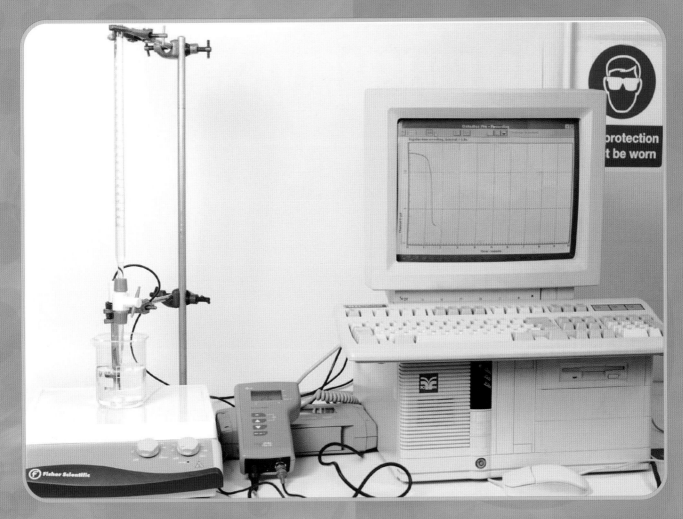

This pH meter shows a pH less than seven. The liquid is an acid.

Make a pH Indicator!

Red cabbage contains a material that makes an acid-base indicator. Place two cups of chopped red cabbage in a blender, cover with boiling water, and blend. Use a coffee filter to filter out the plant material. Add the indicator to materials like lemon juice, baking soda, antacids, and seltzer water. The indicator will turn red/purple/violet in the presence of acids and blue/green/yellow for bases.

Scientists use many indicators for acids and bases in the lab, but you can use cabbage juice to make an acid indicator.

Properties of Acids

You have already learned some of the properties of acids. Let's summarize so you can remember them!

Acids release a hydrogen ion (H+) into an aqueous solution, or a solution with water.

Acids can react with bases when they are combined. When an acid and base are combined, the reaction makes two things happen. First, the acid and base make a neutral liquid, water. The pH of water is about seven. You probably know that the chemical formula of water is H_2O. The hydrogen ions in the acid and the hydroxide ions in the base make the water. Another **product** of the reaction between acids and bases is a solid substance, a salt.

Acids can **corrode** metals. The acid eats away at the metal, causing it to weaken or rust.

Acids can turn blue litmus to red. Litmus does not change color at the exact neutral point between acid and base, but the color change is very close to that point. The compound litmus is often added to paper to make litmus paper.

Acids can conduct electricity. The acid in a car battery has to be powerful to run a car! Battery acid is very strong—and dangerous to touch.

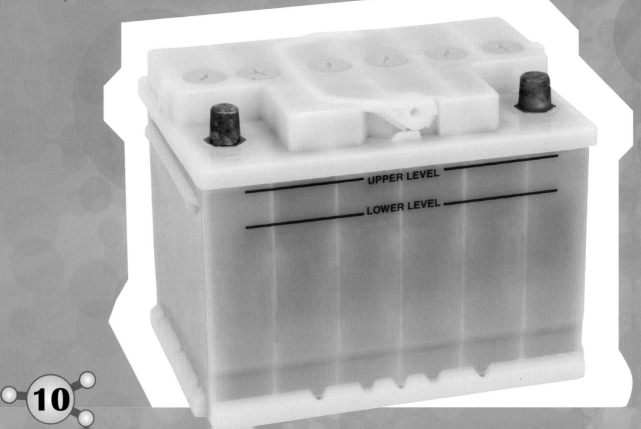

UPPER LEVEL

LOWER LEVEL

Labs include wash stations. If you get acid on your skin, rinse it off immediately. Follow the directions of the person running the lab.

Acids taste sour. The German word for acid is *sauer*. Remember that tasting acids can be extremely dangerous! Do not taste an acid unless a teacher or chemist says that it is safe. You may have tasted sauerkraut. Sauerkraut is cabbage that has been preserved in its own lactic acid. Vinegar is another sour substance in the kitchen. Vinegar has acetic acid that gives it its sour taste.

Strong Acids

You already know that adding an acid to water forms H+ ions. The strongest acids create the most H+ ions. Some of the strong acids are nitric acid, hydrochloric acid, and sulfuric acid. Another strong acid, perchloric acid, will explode if not treated carefully. Strong acids can be corrosive, and they can hurt your skin and the membranes inside your nose and throat.

Properties of Bases

Let's summarize some of the properties of bases!

Bases release a hydroxide ion (OH-) into water. The more ions that are released, the stronger the base.

Do you notice this person is wearing rubber gloves? Never handle strong bases without protection for your skin.

Bases react with acids. When an acid and a base react, they form water and a substance called a salt.

Bases can change the structure of a protein. This property of bases is what makes bases feel slippery. Soap is a base that, when it gets wet, feels very slippery on your skin. This same property—to change the structure of proteins—makes some strong bases very dangerous. Strong bases that will dissolve in water, such as lye, are extremely dangerous, because human skin has many proteins in it. When these strong bases come in contact with skin, they begin to change the structure of the skin. This can cause burns. Strong bases need to be used very carefully to avoid damage to skin.

Bases turn red litmus blue.

Bases have a bitter taste. There are very few foods that are basic, but those that are, such as baking soda, taste bitter rather than sour. Do not taste a substance to see if it is a base unless your teacher or a lab chemist tells you that it is safe. Tasting bases can be even more dangerous than tasting acids because of the damage a base could do to the proteins on your tongue and in your mouth.

These basic solutions are all very useful in our homes.

Strong Bases

Strong bases release many hydroxide ions (OH–) when they are put into an aqueous solution. The strongest bases are created with metals that are in solution with hydroxide ions. You will notice that the names of all these strong bases end with hydroxide—some strong bases are lithium hydroxide, sodium hydroxide, potassium hydroxide, and calcium hydroxide.

What is a Buffer?

A **buffer** is a solution that resists changes in pH when small quantities of acids or bases are added to it. Buffers keep a reaction in **equilibrium**. Here is a simple explanation:

I n a chemical reaction, two or more things come together. These are **reactants**. For example, hydrogen and oxygen are reactants. When they combine, they make water. Water is a product of the reaction. Some systems, though, need to stay in equilibrium—the reactants and products need to stay the same over time. In the reaction to create water, hydrogen and oxygen will keep combining to form water, but not all the reactants will combine. Eventually, a fixed amount of reactants will exist with a fixed amount of products. The reaction will not go into reverse. When the reaction is complete and reactants and products are stable, then the reaction is in equilibrium.

A buffer helps maintain that equilibrium by controlling the pH of the substance in which the chemical reaction takes place. Buffers are extremely important in **organisms** that have many cells. The fluid within a cell and the fluid surrounding a cell have to maintain a constant pH. If the pH changed, the organism could become ill or even die. A buffer keeps the pH constant by not allowing the chemical reaction to go forward or into reverse.

See the man's breath in the cold? A buffer in the body allows carbon dioxide gas to be exhaled from the lungs.

14

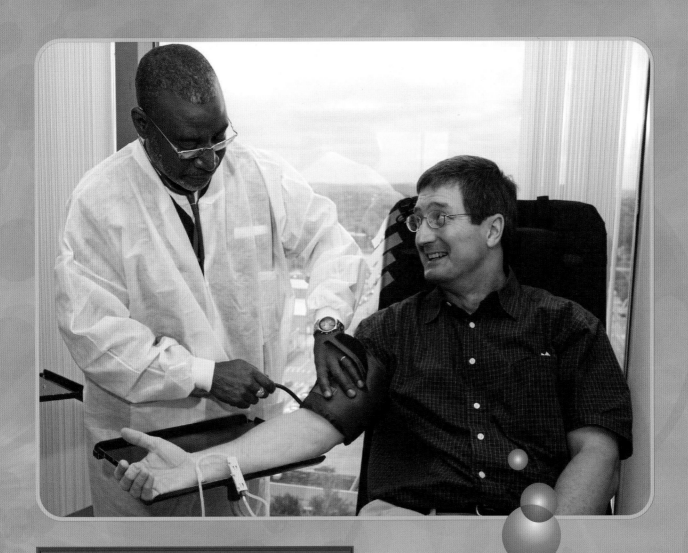

Buffers in Your Body

Buffers regulate the pH of blood. Think about what happens during exercise. Your body uses oxygen and makes carbon dioxide. This produces hydrogen ions in your blood and creates an acid called lactic acid. This means the blood's pH is lowered. To be sure blood stays at the correct pH, a buffer stops chemical reactions from proceeding too far.

Buffers protect the amazing fluid in your body: blood. Why is it so important? Every cell in your body gets nutrients from blood!

Common Acids

What acids do we encounter in our daily lives?
How do we use those acids?

Hydrochloric acid is a strong acid. You should not touch it with your bare skin. But this acid has many uses in our daily lives. When brick-layers put bricks together with mortar, excess mortar may spill or squeeze between bricks.

Hydrochloric acid is strong enough to remove the mortar. This acid also is a strong cleaner around the house, not just at construction sites. It is used to clean swimming pools, and it is even an ingredient in toilet bowl cleaner.

Has biting into a lemon or even an orange made you pucker? Citric acid causes that.

One Acid: Two Surprising Uses!

Have you ever had the vegetable rhubarb? Rhubarb contains an acid called oxalic acid. This acid gives rhubarb a unique taste. Bakers use rhubarb to make pies. Oxalic acid has properties that make it perfect for something very different from baking pies. This same acid can be found in a mechanic's garage to flush out the cooling systems of automobiles.

Sulfuric acid is a strong acid used in chemical manufacturing. This same acid is also used in car batteries. Phosphoric acid is a weaker acid, but it is also a strong cleaner. It can be used to remove lime deposits.

Boric acid, weaker than phosphoric acid, is a major ingredient in solutions used to kill a common household pest—roaches. This same acid is used in some chemical mixtures to fight fires. A mixture of boric acid can be applied to fabrics to make them resistant to fire. Boric acid is the only acid in the world that is beneficial for human eyes rather than harmful. Boric acid is used to treat pink eye and eye infections. Swimmers use boric acid solutions to clean their ears after swimming. Boric acid can treat ear infections in both people and their pets. Boric acid applied to your feet can even make your feet smell better! Powder made from boric acid has a greenish hue that looks great in fireworks.

Soft drinks contain carbonic acid, a weak acid that contributes to the taste and the "bubbles" in soft drinks.

You might have smelled and tasted acetic acid in vinegar, but that same acid might have helped photographers with your school pictures! In some photography labs, acetic acid is a part of the process of developing film. As photographic paper develops, if the photographer sees that the image is perfect exactly as it is, dipping the paper in acetic stops the developing process immediately. The image is preserved, "set" by the acetic acid.

Another common weak acid, citric acid, occurs naturally in citrus fruits like lemons, limes, and oranges. Citric acid is also produced in factories, and it has many uses. Citric acid is used to flavor and preserve food and beverages, especially soft drinks. Citric acid also can work as a water softener. When the acid is added to laundry soaps, its special properties help soaps clean better, even with hard water. The same acid used to flavor soft drinks makes part of a great bathroom or kitchen cleaner. Citric acid is even used to keep fat globules separate in ice cream, which makes the texture smooth and creamy in each bite. You can bathe in water treated with bath salts that contain citric acid. It is interesting to think that the same acid that makes you feel good in the bath makes your ice cream taste creamy!

Baking power actually has an acid and a base. When liquid is added, bubbles are released. Baked goods like muffins and biscuits then rise.

Pickling Metal

When you think of pickles, you might think of sour cucumbers, but pickling is a process that treats metal. In pickling, metal surfaces are treated to remove stains, rust, or scale. The solution used to remove these impurities from the metal is made with one type of acid—either hydrochloric or sulfuric acid. Nitric and hydrofluoric acids can also be used in pickling metal.

Sulfuric acid is used in the chemical reaction that creates gasoline.

Acids in Our Bodies

By now, you probably realize that not all acids are dangerous. Some acids, in fact, are healthy for us.

If you look on the side of the cereal box, you might see folic acid listed as an added ingredient. Folic acid is also found in green leafy vegetables. Studies have shown that folic acid actually improves your body's ability to create new cells. Folic acid may prevent serious illnesses like strokes, cancer, and heart disease. Pregnant women should get folic acid to prevent problems with their babies.

Folic acid is just one of many nutrients that you can add to your body to make you healthier. But what acids are in your body already?

Nucleic acids are essential for all living organisms. They help cells replicate, or copy themselves, and they build protein in the body. DNA, the material that contains all the "instructions" that help organisms grow and develop, is a nucleic acid.

Amino acids are essential for life, too. There are over 20 different amino acids, and every cell in your body uses amino acids to build proteins. Proteins are part of your muscles, and they keep cell walls strong.

Another acid in your body is gastric acid. Gastric acid is made in the walls of your stomach. It is a mixture of hydrochloric acid and other materials that help digest food. It has a pH between one and two, making it a strong acid.

The protein in meats has amino acids. When you eat these foods, you help build amino acids in your body.

Lactic Acid

Lactic acid is in milk products such as yogurt and cottage cheese. The acid gives these foods their sour taste. Cooks may use lactic acid to control a food's pH. Lactic acid can also preserve foods.

Gastric acid helps this girl digest a healthy meal. If too much acid is produced, an antacid base can balance the effects of the acid.

Environmental Acids

Just as a strong acid can corrode metal, acid can have other negative effects on our environment. In a forest, you may see areas of dead trees. In a city, you may see stone buildings worn away. All of these can be caused by **acid rain.**

Two materials that come from power plants, cars, and factories are sulfur dioxide and nitrogen oxide. When these materials enter the atmosphere, they react with water vapor. You already know that most acids are aqueous solutions. The mixture of these materials and water is an acid. This acid can become smog or fall to the ground as rain or sleet.

Even "normal" rain is acidic because of the carbon dioxide in the atmosphere. Rain's pH is 5.6. The pH of acid rain is between 4.3 and 5.0. This pH is about the same as black coffee or orange juice. But that doesn't mean that acid rain is safe. Even the weakest acid rain can kill the eggs of aquatic animals or stop plants from growing.

Smog and acid rain have some of the same "ingredients," but smog does different kinds of damage. It is especially dangerous for people who have trouble breathing.

Acid rain can jeopardize forests by making some of the nutrients in the soil go away. How could this affect our lives?

When acid rain falls to Earth, surface waters are affected the most. Water plants and some animals are killed. Animals that eat the water plants die as their food sources are decreased. Forests die as nutrients in the soil are depleted by the acid rain. Finally, acid rain can erode stone and metal. Acid rain can even destroy paint on cars.

Reducing Acid Rain

How can we reduce the effects of acid rain? New laws limit how much sodium dioxide and nitrous oxides can enter the environment from factories. Car manufacturers are making designs that remove some of these compounds from the exhaust. Solar, nuclear, and water energy do not cause acid rain.

How We Use Bases

Let's take a look at bases and how they affect our lives.

You already know that strong bases are dangerous for your skin. These strong bases are often great cleaning products for our households. Sodium hydroxide, which is also known as lye, is extremely damaging to human skin. But it is also extremely useful. Sodium hydroxide is used to make soap, fabric, and paper. This base is also used to refine petroleum to make gasoline.

One common product with sodium hydroxide is drain cleaner. How does it work? Most drains are clogged with combinations of fat and grease. The sodium hydroxide in drain cleaner takes these fats and greases and changes them into soaps. The soaps dissolve in water. The dissolving of sodium hydroxide in water also creates heat. The heat can actually melt through the clog. That's one reason you need to be very careful with drain cleaner.

If you pour it into a sink already full with water, the heat can boil the water backed up by the pipe and cause it to quickly splash out. Some drain cleaners have another secret weapon—very small pieces of aluminum. The aluminum reacts with the sodium hydroxide in water, and the reaction makes bubbles of hydrogen gas. Those bubbles help get rid of the clog.

> **Bases are widely used as cleaning products, from laundry soap to bathroom cleaners.**

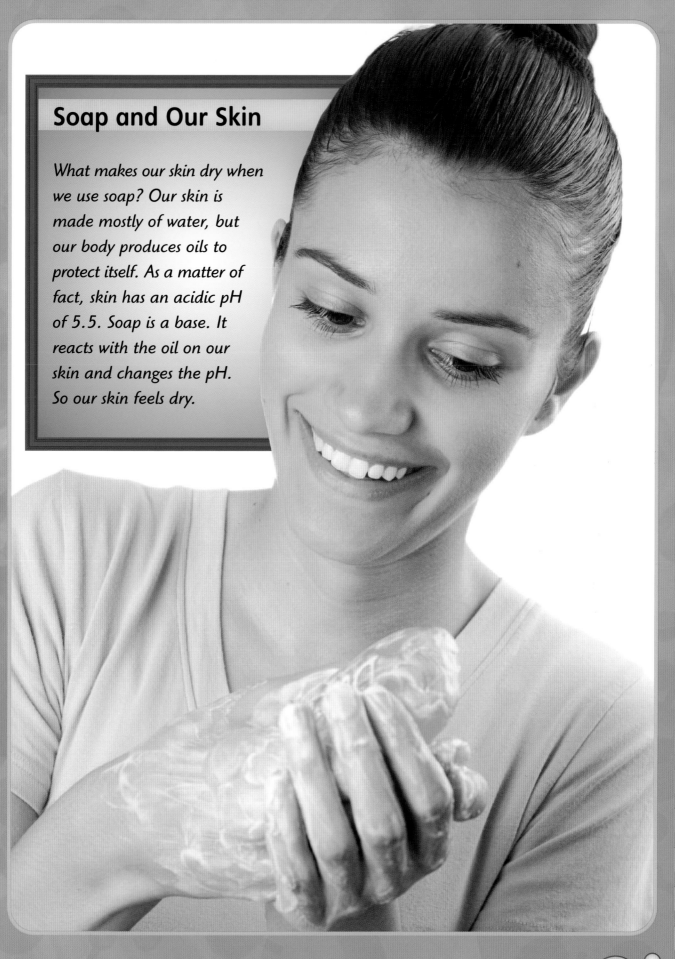

Soap and Our Skin

What makes our skin dry when we use soap? Our skin is made mostly of water, but our body produces oils to protect itself. As a matter of fact, skin has an acidic pH of 5.5. Soap is a base. It reacts with the oil on our skin and changes the pH. So our skin feels dry.

Ammonia is a compound that creates a base when it is mixed with water. Household ammonia is used as a cleaning product. Ammonia can also be used as a fuel. During World War II, fuel shortages caused some countries, such as Belgium, to use ammonia rather than gasoline. Ammonia is not as powerful as many other fuels, but it also leaves much less pollution than fossil fuels. Ammonia can be used as fertilizer. It's especially good for growing crops that need nitrogen in the soil, such as corn.

How can a base help flowers grow? If the pH of the soil is too low, the gardener can add lime, or calcium oxide, to the soil.

If you eat bread, you have eaten a weak base, baking soda. In cooking, the reaction between the baking soda and water releases carbon dioxide. Carbon dioxide is a gas. The release of the gas helps the baked item "rise." Want to make baked goods rise higher and faster? An acid in the recipe will increase that reaction. Acids in recipes could include cream of tartar, lemon juice, yogurt, buttermilk, vinegar, or even cocoa.

Cooking isn't the only place to use baking soda. Baking soda may be used to put out a small fire. Made into a paste, baking soda is effective for scrubbing things. A process for blasting paint off of surfaces uses baking soda. Baking soda can remove smells from a refrigerator; and the substance is even a tool against global warming, because it can trap greenhouse gas emissions.

How Does Antacid Work?

Hydrochloric acid, found in the lining of the stomach, is necessary to properly digest food. A person who eats too much of a certain food or has a weak stomach lining may end up with too much acid in the stomach. An antacid is a base that neutralizes the extra acid.

Baking soda is a base that helps baked goods "rise."

Chemical Reactions

What happens when you put an acid and a base together? In a reaction in which an acid and a base are reactants, the products are a salt and water. The materials used to create the salt and the water come from the acid and the base.

A titration is a special kind of experiment in which researchers can find the pH of an unknown liquid by comparing it to a known liquid.

The pH of water is right around seven, so water is neutral—it is neither an acid nor a base. Because water forms from the reaction between acids and bases, this reaction between an acid and a base is also called a **neutralization** reaction.

Common table salt is created from a reaction between an acid and a base. When hydrochloric acid and sodium hydroxide are combined, one of the products is water. The other product is sodium chloride, the chemical name for the salt we use in cooking.

When you do any experiments with acids or bases in the lab, be very careful. If you are mixing a strong acid with water, for example, start with the water and then add acid. Why? If you instead pour water into sulfuric acid, for example, the solution will boil and can "spit" sulfuric acid, which can burn your skin. If you add acid to the water, the acid is heavier and will sink. Any reactions that could hurt you will happen inside the container rather than outside.

Make a Volcano!

Make dough with 6 cups flour, 2 cups salt, 4 tablespoons of cooking oil, and 2 cups water. Mold the dough around a soda bottle. Fill 2/3 of the bottle with water, a few drops of food coloring, and 6 drops of detergent. Add 2 tablespoons of baking soda into the bottle. Both the detergent and baking soda are bases. Now slowly pour vinegar, an acid, into the bottle. What happens?

Glossary

acid A compound usually having a sour taste and capable of neutralizing bases and turning blue litmus paper red, containing hydrogen ion

acid rain Precipitation that contains high concentrations of acid-forming chemicals

alkali Any of various bases, the hydroxides of alkali metals and ammonium

aqueous Of, like, or containing water

atom The smallest component of an element having the chemical properties of the element

base A compound that reacts with an acid to form a salt

buffer A substance that, added to a solution, is capable of neutralizing acids and bases without changing the acidity or alkalinity of the solution

corrode To wear away gradually, especially by chemical action

electron An elementary particle that is part of matter, having a negative charge

equilibrium The condition when a chemical reaction and its reverse reaction are at equal rates

gas A substance that can expand

ion An atom or group of atoms with a positive or negative charge

liquid A substance that expands to take the shape of its container

matter The substance or substances of which any physical object consists or is composed

neutral Having the properties of neither an acid or a base